The # Uniqueness
of Jesus

The Life & Teachings of Jesus

INTRODUCTION

Bill Bright

*New*Life
PUBLICATIONS
A MINISTRY OF CAMPUS CRUSADE FOR CHRIST

Ten Basic Steps Toward Christian Maturity
Introduction: The Uniqueness of Jesus

Published by
NewLife Publications
100 Sunport Lane
Orlando, FL 32809

Printed in the United States of America.

ISBN: 1-56399-029-6

Thomas Nelson Inc., Nashville, Tennessee, is the exclusive distributor of this book to the trade markets in the United States and the District of Columbia.

Distributed in Canada by Campus Crusade for Christ of Canada, Surrey, B.C.

Unless otherwise indicated, all Scripture references are from the *New International Version*, © 1973, 1978, 1984 by the International Bible Society. Published by Zondervan Bible Publishers, Grand Rapids, Michigan.

Scripture quotations designated TLB are from *The Living Bible*, © 1971 by Tyndale House Publishers, Wheaton, Illinois.

Scripture quotations designated Phillips are from *Letters to Young Churches, A Translation of the New Testament Epistles*, by J. B. Phillips, © 1947, 1957 by the MacMillan Company, New York, New York.

Any royalties from this book or the many other books by Bill Bright are dedicated to the glory of God and designated to the various ministries of Campus Crusade for Christ/*NewLife2000*.

For more information, write:

Life Ministries—P. O. Box 40, Flemington Markets, N5W 2129, Australia
Campus Crusade for Christ of Canada—Box 300, Vancouver, B.C., V6C 2X3, Canada
Campus Crusade for Christ—Fairgate House, King's Road, Tyseley, Birmingham, B11 2AA, England
Campus Crusade for Christ—P. O. Box 8786, Auckland, New Zealand
Campus Crusade for Christ—Alexandra, P. O. Box 0205, Singapore 9115, Singapore
Great Commission Movement of Nigeria—P. O. Box 500, Jos, Plateau State Nigeria, West Africa
Campus Crusade for Christ International—100 Sunport Lane, Orlando, FL 32809, USA

Contents

Acknowledgments

The *Ten Basic Steps Toward Christian Maturity* series was a product of necessity. As the ministry of Campus Crusade for Christ expanded rapidly to scores of campuses across America, thousands of students committed their lives to Christ—several hundred on a single campus. Individual follow-up of all new converts soon became impossible. Who was to help them grow in their new-found faith?

A Bible study series designed for new Christians was desperately needed—a study that would stimulate individuals and groups to explore the depths and the riches of God's Word. Although several excellent studies were available, we felt the particular need of new material for these college students.

In 1955, I asked several of my fellow staff associates to assist me in the preparation of Bible studies that would stimulate both evangelism and Christian growth in a new believer. The contribution by campus staff members was especially significant because of their constant contact with students in introducing them to Christ and meeting regularly with them to disciple them. Thus, the *Ten Basic Steps Toward Christian Maturity* was the fruit of our combined labor.

Since that modest beginning, many other members of the staff have contributed generously. On occasion, for example, I found myself involved in research and writing sessions with several of our staff, all seminary graduates, some with advanced degrees and one with his doctorate in theology. More important, all were actively engaged in "winning, building, and sending men" for Christ.

For this latest edition, I want to thank Don Tanner for his professional assistance in revising, expanding, and editing the contents. I also want to thank Joette Whims and Jean Bryant for their extensive help and for joining Don and me in the editorial process.

A Personal Word

In 1946 when Jesus Christ became my Savior, Lord, and Master, there was little cooperation and communication between denominational churches and ministry specialist (parachurch) groups. Organizations such as Navigators, Intervarsity, Young Life, and Youth for Christ were not warmly received. The "walls" of division were high and thick.

Since that time a miracle has occurred. Today there is a growing spirit of harmony and love. Most church members are less concerned about the denominations, and parachurch groups are more universally respected, received, and appreciated. The walls are tumbling down!

In fact, the greatest spiritual awakening of all time is taking place today. More people are hearing the gospel; more people are receiving Christ; more people are committed to helping fulfill the Great Commission than at any other time since the church was born almost 2,000 years ago.

Here in the United States, one-third of all adults identify themselves as born-again, evangelical Christians. More than 100 million attend church each Sunday and more millions listen to Christian radio and television programs regularly.

But we have a serious problem. These facts are not reflected in the life of our nation.

According to our surveys, fewer than 50 percent of the church members in America are sure of their salvation, only 5 percent understand the ministry of the Holy Spirit, and a bare 2 percent regularly share their faith in Christ. Obviously something is tragically wrong.

Our Lord has commanded us to be the salt of the earth and the light of the world, but in spite of the fact that Christians represent a large segment of the American population, we have a negligible influence in government, education, media, or any other facet of our society. There is need for a great spiritual revival and revolution in America, and throughout the world. To influence the world effectively for Christ, a great body of Christians must be growing spiritually, introducing men and women to the Savior, and helping other believers reach a higher level of Christian maturity. The individual Christian must be committed to living a holy life and to reaching his or her own community with the gospel.

An in-depth study of God's Word is a major factor in accomplishing these things. The *Ten Basic Steps Toward Christian Maturity* course—composed of this Introduction plus ten dynamic Steps to walking with Christ and living a joyful, victorious life—has been written to facilitate that type of study.

Designed originally to help college students explore the riches of God's Word, the course has been equally effective with adults and young people in churches, home Bible study groups, military and prison facilities, and in many high schools.

Now, the entire work, including the *Ten Basic Steps Toward Christian Maturity Leader's Guide,* has been revised, expanded and updated. It can be used for personal as well as group Bible study and is very effective for any Christian who wants to grow spiritually.

This course has been prepared so that, when used with the *Leader's Guide,* even an inexperienced, first-time teacher can lead a Bible study successfully.

The lesson material in the booklets also has been combined in a single paperback volume called *A Handbook for Christian Maturity.*

My prayer is that these studies will greatly bless and enrich your life, and that you will be further encouraged in your growth toward full maturity in Jesus Christ. I trust also that the effectiveness of your personal witness for Him will be greatly enhanced.

Bill Bright

What This Study Will Do for You

Who would you say is the central figure of all history? Most people, believers and non-believers alike, would say Jesus.

If you have wondered why Jesus is such a unique and dominant figure in history, you will be excited about *The Uniqueness of Jesus*. This study is the Introduction to the *Ten Basic Steps Toward Christian Maturity*, a time-tested study series designed to provide you with a sure foundation for your faith.

You will benefit from this introductory study in two ways:

First, *by learning who Jesus Christ really is.*

Jesus is the most remarkable and fascinating person in history. When He walked this earth, He stirred people wherever He went. This study presents the person of Jesus Christ: who He is, His earthly life, His death, and His resurrection and continuing ministry in the lives of all believers.

In this study, you will gain a better understanding of His nature. You will discover why the life of this one person, and the church He established, sparked an explosive movement that has dramatically changed society through the centuries.

Second, *by understanding what He has done for you.*

As you view the privileges and responsibilities of the Christian life, you will discover

❖

A faithful study of the *Ten Basic Steps* will show you how to walk daily in the power of the Holy Spirit.

8

the secret of His power to transform you and give you a continually abundant and fruitful life. You will learn what it means to surrender totally to Christ and let Him live His life in and through you.

As you apply the principles you learn in this study, you will sense changes coming into your life. You will learn how to receive Christ as your Savior and Lord, and you will be given an opportunity to invite Him into your life if you have not already done so.

Foundation for Faith

The *Ten Basic Steps* course, when used during your personal quiet times or in a group setting, can give you an efficient way to study the Bible and understand the Christian faith.

The *Ten Basic Steps* study is divided into eleven parts, with an individual booklet for the introductory study and one for each of the ten Steps. These study guides correlate with the expanded and updated *Handbook for Christian Maturity* and the *Ten Basic Steps Leader's Guide*.

When you complete the introductory Step, I encourage you to go on to Step 1 and continue through the series until you have completed Step 10. Study the lessons diligently and review each of the Steps periodically to make the principles you learn your own.

If you are a new Christian, the *Ten Basic Steps* will acquaint you with the major doctrines of the Christian faith. By applying the principles you will learn, you will grow spiritually and find solutions to problems you are likely to face as a new believer.

If you are a mature Christian, you will discover the tools you need to help others receive Christ and grow in their faith. Your own commitment to our Lord will be affirmed, and you will discover how to develop an effective devotional and study plan.

A faithful study of the *Ten Basic Steps Toward Christian Maturity* will also show you how to walk daily in the power of the Holy Spirit, enabling you to live a more joyous and triumphant Christian life.

You are about to begin one of the most life-changing Bible studies ever developed. Millions of people throughout the world today are following Jesus Christ and experiencing the power of His resurrection because this study helped them to build a strong foundation for their faith.

How to Use This Study

On page 13 of this Introduction, you will find the preparatory article, "The Uniqueness of Jesus." The article will give you a clear perspective on who Jesus is. Read it carefully before proceeding with the individual lessons.

The Introduction contains six lessons plus a "Recap" or review. At the end of some of the steps you will find supplementary material. Be sure to read this and make its principles your own.

Each lesson is divided into two sections: the Bible Study and the Life Application. Begin by noting the Objective for the lesson you are studying. The Objective states the main goal for your study. Keep it in mind as you continue through the lesson.

Appropriate memory verses have been provided to help you in your walk with Christ. Learn each verse by writing it on a small card to carry with you. You can buy cards for these verses at any bookstore or print shop, or you can make your own by using filing cards. Review daily the verses you have memorized.

I cannot overemphasize the importance of memorizing Bible verses. Our Lord has commanded that we learn His Word. Proverbs 7:1–3 reminds us:

Give God a chance to speak to you, and let the Holy Spirit teach you.

My son, keep my words and store up my commands within you. Keep my commands and you will live; guard my teachings as the apple of your eye. Bind them on your fingers; write them on the tablet of your heart.

As you meditate on the verses you have memorized and claim God's promises, you will experience the joy, victory, and power that God's Word gives to your Christian walk. When you have finished all the studies in the entire series, you will be able to develop your own Bible study, continuing to use a systematic method for memorizing God's Word.

How to Study the Lessons

Casual Bible reading uncovers valuable spiritual facts that lie near the surface. But understanding the deeper truths requires study. Often the difference between reading and studying is a pen and notepad.

Every lesson in this series covers an important topic and gives you an opportunity to record your answers to the questions. Plan to spend a minimum of thirty minutes each day—preferably in the morning—in Bible study, meditation, and prayer.

Remember, the most important objective and benefit of a quiet time or Bible study is not to acquire knowledge or accumulate biblical information but to meet with God in a loving, personal way.

Here are some suggestions to help you in your study time:

◆ Plan a specific time and place to work on these studies. Make an appointment with God, then keep it.

◆ Have a pen or pencil, your Bible, and this booklet.

◆ Begin with prayer for God's presence, blessing, and wisdom.

◆ Meditate on the Objective to determine how it fits into your circumstances.

◆ Memorize the suggested verses.

◆ Proceed to the Bible Study, trusting God to use it to teach you. Prayerfully anticipate His presence with you. Work carefully, reading the Scripture passages and thinking through the questions. Answer each as completely as possible.

◆ When you come to the Life Application, answer the questions honestly and begin to apply them to your own life.

◆ Prayerfully read through the lesson again and reevaluate your Life Application answers. Do they need changing? Or adjusting?

◆ Review the memory verses.

◆ Consider the Objective again and determine if it has been accomplished. If not, what do you need to do?

◆ Close with a prayer of thanksgiving, and ask God to help you grow spiritually in the areas He has specifically revealed to you.

◆ When you complete the first six lessons of this Introduction, spend extra time on the Recap to make sure you understand every lesson thoroughly.

◆ If you feel you need more study, ask God for wisdom again and go through whatever lesson(s) you need to review, repeating the process until you do understand and are able to apply the truths to your own life.

These studies are not intended as a complete development of Christian beliefs. However, a careful study of the material will give you, with God's help, a sufficient understanding of how you can know and apply God's plan for your life. The spiritual truths contained here will help you meet with our Lord Jesus Christ in an intimate way and discover the full and abundant life that Jesus promised (John 10:10).

Do not rush through the lessons. Take plenty of time to think through the questions. Meditate on them. Absorb the truths presented, and make the application a part of your life. Give God a chance to speak to you, and let the Holy Spirit teach you. As you spend time with our Lord in prayer and study, and as you trust and obey Him, you will experience the amazing joy of His presence (John 14:21).

The Uniqueness of Jesus

Some time ago, a brilliant young medical student from another land, a follower of an Eastern religion, came to see me. Through the preceding months, we had become good friends.

I asked this young man several questions: "In your opinion, who is the greatest leader the world has ever known? Who has done the most good for mankind?"

After a moment of hesitation, he replied, "I'm sure Jesus has done more good than anyone who has ever lived. I would say He is the greatest leader."

Then I asked, "Who do you think is the greatest teacher?"

No doubt he considered Socrates, Aristotle, Plato, Confucius, and other great philosophers of ancient and modern times. But he answered, "The greatest teacher is Jesus."

Finally I asked, "Who in the entire history of man do you believe has lived the most holy life?"

Immediately he answered, "There has never been anyone like Jesus."

❖

No other person in history has influenced the world for good more than Jesus Christ.

I have posed these questions to knowledgeable people of all religions, as well as atheists and Communists. The answer is always the same: "Jesus."

Indeed, there has never been anyone who could compare with Jesus of Nazareth. He is unique among all human beings.

Worldwide Influence

No other person in history has influenced the world for good more than Jesus Christ. His life and message have greatly changed the lives of people and nations. History is His Story, the story of the life of one man. Remove Jesus of Nazareth from history, and it would be a completely different account.

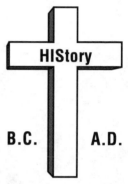

For the past 2,000 years, He has been the centerpiece of humanity. Charles Spurgeon, an English theologian, wrote:

> Christ is the great central fact in the world's history. To him everything looks forward of backward. All the lines of history converge upon him. All the great purposes of God culminate in him. The greatest and most momentous fact which the history of the world records is the fact of his birth.[1]

Consider today's date on your calendar. It gives witness to the fact that Jesus of Nazareth, the Christ, lived on this earth. "B.C." means "before Christ"; "A.D." is the abbreviation of *anno Domini*, the Latin phrase that is translated "in the year of our Lord."

Jesus has influenced the whole world. The New Testament declares that in Christ there is neither male nor female, slave nor free. Wherever Christ has gone, human worth and personal rights have been recognized and encouraged.

Also, institutions of higher learning and facilities for medical care have been established; child labor laws have been enacted;

---

[1] Sherwood Eliot Wirt and Kersten Beckstrom, *Living Quotations for Christians* (New York: Harper & Row Publishers, 1974), No. 1749.

slavery has been abolished; and a multitude of other changes have been made for the good of mankind.

It would be impossible to show the magnitude of Christ's influence on the world. I can only help you step closer to the mural of history to examine a few of the ways in which His life and message have made a dramatic difference in civilization.

Social reform

Jesus fed the hungry, healed the sick, comforted the bereaved, and loved the outcast.

Hundreds of millions of believers through the centuries have followed His example. The more serious the social problems, the greater the desire of Christian men and women to find remedies for these ills.

From the beginning, the followers of Jesus treated individuals with dignity and worth unknown to their pagan culture. As a result, wherever missionaries took the true gospel of Christ, social conditions dramatically improved and cultures were enriched.

Christians established hospitals and schools, moved for prison reform, established orphanages, provided famine relief, raised the status of women, and worked to abolish cruel social customs, including cannibalism and human sacrifice. Other Christian leaders, such as William Booth, who founded the Salvation Army, began endeavors to relieve human suffering in urban areas.

Today, committed Christian believers are fighting to halt abortion and euthanasia; they are working diligently to reduce child abuse, drug addiction, and alcoholism; they are seeking to eliminate pornography, and are taking a stand against homosexuality. Christian organizations are coordinating actions against age-old problems such as prejudice, poverty, gang violence, crime, famine, and family dysfunction.

Medicine

Jesus Christ also felt compassion for those who suffered from disease and handicaps. He cured the leper, healed the lame, and gave sight to the blind. In the process, He taught His disciples to show the same compassion.

Believers have cared for the sick ever since the time of Christ. The Red Cross, founded by Christians, rose to care for the ill, encourage public health education, and relieve suffering. For multitudes of disadvantaged people today, Christians bring the love of Christ in word and deed through medical relief.

Business

The principles Jesus taught have made an impact on the world of business. The early church taught the dignity of labor, and believers were admonished to work hard and to shun laziness. During the Middle Ages, monasteries improved agriculture by increasing crop yields and developing methods of tillage. The church also insisted on a just price for goods and fair wages for the worker.

The Reformation inspired dramatic changes in the world of business. By emphasizing every vocation as a "call" from God, Christians encouraged the growth of a new urban middle class.

In more modern times, under the leadership of John Wesley and George Whitefield, many Christians, individually and in groups, began striving for reform in the workplace. Some fought for regulations to protect women and children in mines and industry. Others opposed forced labor, helped enact child labor laws, and formed labor unions.

And many godly men such as J. L. Kraft of Kraft Cheese and J. C. Penney, who founded a merchandizing empire by that name, built businesses based on biblical principles and sought to make work conditions fair and profitable for their employees.

Science

Christianity has had a profound influence upon science as well. The biblical view of an orderly and dependable universe formed and held together by a divine Creator became the foundation for many of history's scientific discoveries.

Christ's teaching inspired the thinking of many celebrated forerunners of modern science, including Roger Bacon, Nicolaus Copernicus, Johannes Kepler, Galileo, Blaise Pascal, and Isaac Newton. Christian thought also was foundational to applied science—fostering industrialization, medical progress, space research, and advances in other scientific fields.

Although during the 19th and 20th centuries many scientists tried to separate science and religion, recent discoveries and developments have shown the emptiness of science without Christ. Today, an increasing number of scientists are joining a long list of famous forerunners who have embraced a biblical faith in Christ.

Law and government

Christian principles have had a significant effect on law and government. The early Christians promoted justice. Converted politicians worked for legislation on behalf of widows, orphans, and the poor, and against immoral and harsh practices. Christ's influence strengthened resistance to barbaric invasion and brought orderly living to pagan tribes.

English common law was developed from the idea that man is accountable to a higher law based on the Bible. Similarly, biblical principles of freedom and justice provide a basis for the Constitution of the United States.

Arts and culture

Christian ideals are reflected in art and culture. The early Christians redirected the pagan focus of the arts where they lived. Beginning with the New Testament, believers created a vital new body of literature in a dying Roman civilization. By the 6th century, the arts were preserved and developed almost exclusively within the church.

After the Reformation, artists were inspired by many different Christian schools of thought. Lutheranism introduced a new hymnody; Roman Catholicism influenced Rembrandt; Michelangelo, Leonardo DiVinci, and Raphael expressed biblical themes in their art and sculpture.

The dynamic spiritual music of Bach, Beethoven, and Handel rings down through the ages. John Bunyan, Dante, and Milton created their literature around scriptural motifs. Even artists who claimed no allegiance to Jesus Christ used Christian symbols and imagery in their work.

Education

One of the most consistent and important influences of Jesus Christ lies in education. In the first centuries, the church took upon itself the task of increasing literacy so that every believer could read the words of Jesus.

During the Dark Ages, the church alone maintained schools, founded universities that became seats of intellectual activity, and developed great libraries. Eventually the Reformation brought learning to the masses, and literacy spread among women. A reconstruction of educational methods and curriculum resulted. Hundreds of Christian colleges were established—many of which are listed today among the most prestigious institutions in the world.

Wherever Christian missionaries settled, a rise in literacy followed. These devout believers gave written form to hundreds of languages and taught millions of people to read and write. Today, many mission groups continue their work in disadvantaged areas of the world.

The influence of Jesus is still revolutionizing our world. Christianity has spanned cultural diversities, prejudice barriers, and political differences.

Personal Influence

I have visited hundreds of campuses around the world and talked to hundreds of thousands of college men and women about Jesus Christ. I have met professors and students alike who were militantly antagonistic toward Him. Some of them contended that He is a myth or that He is a great man and nothing more. Later, however, some of these same people have, out of intellectual honesty, reversed their thinking and become followers of Jesus.

I was deeply moved while reading about one such scholar in the magazine section of the *Los Angeles Times* early one Sunday morning in 1953. My eye fell on a picture of a venerable old professor, Dr. Cyril E. M. Joad, and the dramatic story of the change that had taken place in his life.

One of the world's greatest philosophers, Dr. Joad was for years head of the Philosophy Department at the University of London. He and his colleagues—Julian Huxley, Bertrand Russell, H. G. Wells, and George Bernard Shaw—had probably done more to undermine the faith of the collegiate world of the last generation than any other group.

Dr. Joad believed that Jesus was only a man and that God was a part of the universe. Should the universe be destroyed, he taught, God would also be destroyed. He believed that there is no such thing as sin and that man was essentially good and was destined for utopia.

The article described the many years he had been antagonistic toward Christianity and how he denied the existence of sin. However, he said that two world wars and the imminence of another had conclusively demonstrated to him that man was indeed sinful. Now he believed that the only explanation for sin was found in the Bible and that the only solution for sin was the cross of Jesus Christ. Before his death, Dr. Joad became a zealous follower of Christ.

Only Explanation   **Only Solution**

Another example is Lew Wallace, a famous general and a literary genius. He set out to write a book that would forever destroy the myth of Christianity. Mr. Wallace tells how he spent two years in leading libraries of Europe and America looking for information for the book. Before he finished the second chapter, he found himself on his knees crying out to Jesus saying, "My Lord, and my God." The evidence proving the deity of Jesus that he discovered overwhelmingly convinced him that Jesus Christ was the Son of God, the only Savior of man. Later Lew Wallace wrote *Ben Hur*, one of the greatest novels ever written concerning the time of Christ.

Consider, too, the example of C. S. Lewis. A writer and professor at Oxford and Cambridge Universities in England, he was an agnostic for years. He tried to convince himself that Christianity was invalid. But after a long process of searching for answers, he received Christ as his own Savior and Lord while he was at Oxford. He describes that moment:

> You must picture me alone in that room in Magdalen, night after night, feeling whenever my mind lifted for even a second from my work, the steady, unrelenting

approach of Him whom I so earnestly desired not to meet. That which I greatly feared had at last come upon me. In the Trinity Term of 1929 I gave in, and admitted that God was God, and knelt and prayed: perhaps that night, the most dejected and reluctant convert in all England.[2]

C. S. Lewis became a devout follower of Jesus and wrote many books advocating his belief in Christ. In *Mere Christianity*, he writes:

You can shut Him up for a fool, you can spit at Him and kill Him as a demon; or you can fall at His feet and call Him Lord and God. But let us not come up with any patronizing nonsense about His being a great human teacher. He has not left that open to us. He did not intend to.[3]

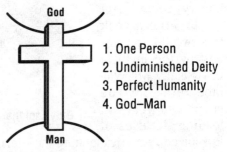

C. S. Lewis concluded that Jesus is indeed more than a good moral teacher: He is the Savior of the world.

1. One Person
2. Undiminished Deity
3. Perfect Humanity
4. God–Man

Who is Jesus of Nazareth to you? A myth? A mere man? Or the Son of God? Your response to these questions will determine your eternal destiny—and the quality of life you can experience on this earth.

The Son of God

People sometimes ask, "Is Christianity really established on historical facts?" When I talk about Christ to great scholars today, I am appalled to find that many of them do not believe Jesus is the Son of God, our Savior. Nearly always, these man are ignorant of the basic truths of the gospel. They take issue with something that they do not fully understand.

---

[2] C. S. Lewis, *Surprised by Joy: The Shape of My Early Life* (New York: Harcourt and Brace, 1966) pp. 228,229.

[3] C. S. Lewis, *Mere Christianity* (New York: The MacMillan Company, 1960), pp. 40,41.

But I have yet to meet a person who has honestly considered the overwhelming evidence proving the deity of Jesus of Nazareth who does not admit that He is the Son of God.

Yes, I have met some who do not believe that Jesus is the Son of God. But as we have talked and reasoned together, they have been honest in confessing, "I have not taken the time to read the Bible or to consider the historical facts concerning Jesus."

Their rejection and sometimes resentment of Christ has inevitably been based upon a lack of knowledge, an unfortunate emotional experience, the inconsistency of some Christian, or perhaps upon the influence of a high school teacher or college professor. Yet they have always admitted that they have not honestly considered the person of Jesus Christ and His claim on their lives.

God's Word provides abundant testimony to the deity of Christ. Paul writes in Colossians 1:13–17,20:

> [God] has rescued us out of the darkness and gloom of Satan's kingdom and brought us into the kingdom of his dear Son, who bought our freedom with his blood and forgave us all our sins.
>
> Christ is the exact likeness of the unseen God. He existed before God made anything at all, and, in fact, Christ himself is the Creator who made everything in heaven and earth, the things we can see and the things we can't...all were made by Christ for his own use and glory. He was before all else began and it is his power that holds everything together.
>
> It was through what his Son did that God cleared a path for everything to come to him—all things in heaven and on earth—for Christ's death on the cross has made peace with God for all by his blood (TLB).

Hebrews 1:1–3 records:

> Long ago God spoke in many different ways to our fathers through the prophets [in visions,

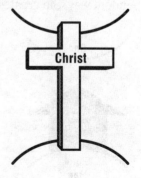

dreams, and even face to face], telling them little by little about his plans.

But now in these days he has spoken to us through his Son to whom he has given everything, and through whom he made the world and everything there is.

God's Son shines out with God's glory, and all that God's Son is and does marks him as God. He regulates the universe by the mighty power of his command. He is the one who died to cleanse us and clear our record of all sin, and then sat down in highest honor beside the great God of heaven (TLB).

Jesus Christ, the Son of God, is the only answer to our world's needs today. There are many things that He can do for us that no one else can do. Here I want to concentrate on four specific things.

First, Jesus is the only one who can *pardon* us from our sin. Second, He alone gives *purpose* for life. Third, only He can give us *peace* when our heart is troubled. Finally, He alone can give us *power* to live an abundant life.

Jesus Alone Can Pardon Us From Sin

The Bible proclaims that God is *holy* and that man is *sinful*. The psalmist says, "The Lord our God is holy" (Psalm 99:9). The apostle records, "All have sinned and fall short of the glory of God" (Romans 3:23).

Sin is more than lying, stealing, or living an immoral life. It is an *attitude*; it is turning our back on God and going our own independent way. Sin creates a vast gulf between us and God that even

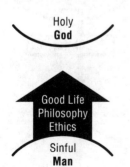

our most noble efforts cannot bridge. This makes it impossible for us to have a personal relationship with Him.

In a careful study of the most popular religions of the world, you would soon become aware that no provision is made for the forgiveness of sin apart from the cross of Jesus Christ. Most religions embrace the philosophy of good works as a means to salvation. Man subscribes to the concept that if his good works outweigh his bad works, he will go to heaven, but if his bad works outweigh his good works, he will go to hell—if there is a hell. Of course, he cannot know until his life is over whether he will go to heaven or to hell. What a tragedy! How inadequate such a religion or philosophy is. But God has promised that we *can* know Him, and have fellowship with Him now and for all eternity, through His Son, the Lord Jesus Christ.

In the Old Testament, the Israelites brought their sacrifices—an unblemished lamb, dove, or bullock—to the priest. The animal was slain, and its blood was sprinkled by the priest on the altar as a temporary covering for sin. This offering pictured the coming of God's one special Lamb, whose blood would not just temporarily cover man's sin, but would wash them away forever.

The fulfillment of this Old Testament picture is recorded in the New Testament. Jesus said:

> O God, the blood of bulls and goats cannot satisfy you, so you have made ready this body of mine for me to lay as a sacrifice upon your altar. You were not satisfied with the animal sacrifices, slain and burnt before you as offerings for sin…See, I have come to do your will, to lay down my life, just as the Scriptures said that I would (Hebrews 10:5–7, TLB).

God sent His only Son, the Lamb of God, without spot or blemish, to shed His blood upon the cross for the forgiveness of our sins. This means that through Jesus Christ, you can know God and have fellowship with Him now and for all eternity.

Even while you were yet a sinner, God loved you enough to send His Son to die on the cross for you that you might have eternal life. Like a prisoner facing certain execution who is suddenly freed, you can be pardoned from your sin through the death and resurrection of Jesus Christ.

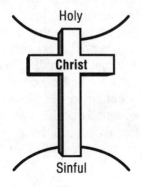

Such love is beyond our human comprehension. God's love is unconditional, undeserved, and based purely on His mercy and grace. He loves us in spite of our disobedience, our weakness, our sin, and our selfishness. Because of His special love, He wants to set us free to live an abundant, joyful life. We need not fear Someone who loves us so perfectly. We can trust Him with our entire life.

Because of His unconditional love, God forgives us absolutely. He cleanses us thoroughly, and He forgets our sins completely.

After I finished speaking at a midwestern university campus, a group of students remained to learn how they could become Christians. Among them was a young Hindu scholar from India who was pacing up and down, angry and impatient. As we talked he said, "I resent you Christians. I resent the arrogance with which you say that you have the only way to God. I believe that Christianity is one way, but only one way. Hinduism is another. Buddhism, Shintoism, and others are all ways to God."

I called his attention to the writings of the great Hindu leader Mahatma Ghandi, who, for all of his devotion to his religion, states in his autobiography, "It is a constant torture to me that I am still so far from Him whom I know to be my very life and being. I know it is my own wretchedness and wickedness that keep me from Him."

This gifted young man said he had once believed that Ghandi was God but, or course, he no longer believed this. In addition to being devout, the young man was unusually brilliant. He was completing a double doctorate—one in physics and another in chemistry.

As we talked together, his anger began to subside, and he began to see that Christianity was different. He saw that it was not just another man-made religion of philosophy, but that it made provision for man's basic need: forgiveness of sin. He admitted also that he had not found the answer to his needs, though he was a devout follower of his religion, diligent in the reading of the sacred Hindu writings, and faithful in his times of prayer and all the rituals of his faith. He had to confess that he had never found God. I called his attention to the difference in the lives of Christian friends. He admitted that they had something he did not possess. It was obvious that that "something" was the Savior who had come to live within them and had forgiven them of their sins.

For nearly an hour we discussed the difference between Christianity and the religions of the world. For example, you can take Buddha out of Buddhism, Mohammed out of Islam, and in like manner the founders of various religions out of their religious systems, and little would be changed. But if you took Christ out of Christianity, nothing would be left.

Biblical Christianity, on the other hand, is not a philosophy of life or a code of ethics. It is a personal relationship with God, the Creator of the universe, who revealed Himself to man through His only begotten Son, the Lord Jesus Christ.

Finally, the light came on, and this young Hindu understood the great truth of pardon for sin through our Savior's sacrifice on the cross. Quietly he bowed his head. This dear young scholar, with all of his heart, now prayed that Jesus of Nazareth—the risen, living Son of God—would come into his heart, pardon his sin, and become his Lord and Master.

The Bible says:

> There is no other name under heaven given to men by which we must be saved (Acts 4:12).

Only Jesus can pardon us from sin.

Jesus Alone Gives Purpose

Not only is Jesus of Nazareth unique as the only one who can *pardon* us from our sins, but He is also unique as the only one who gives *purpose* to life.

Quite likely, at some time you have wondered: Where did I come from? Why am I here? What will happen to me when I die?

True purpose for living has been the quest of mankind since the beginning. Without it, men despair.

For example, the famous historian and philosopher H. G. Wells lamented near the end of his life, "I have no peace. All life is at the end of its tether."

The poet Lord Byron said, "My days are in the yellow leaf, the flowers and fruits of life are gone, the worm and the canker and the grief are mine alone."

Henry David Thoreau, the great literary genius, said, "Most men live lives of quiet desperation."

The famous American cartoonist Ralph Barton left this note pinned to his pillow before he took his own life: "I have had few difficulties, many friends, great successes; I have gone from wife to wife, and from house to house, and visited great countries of the world, but I am fed up with inventing devices to fill up twenty-four hours of the day."

Clearly, neither fame nor success nor wealth can ease the agony of such empty lives. If these things cannot satisfy, how then can we find lasting fulfillment?

No contractor would think of constructing a skyscraper without checking the plans of the architect. Just so, we would be foolish to fashion our lives without first consulting the great Architect of life.

The person who builds his life according to God's plan is promised true purpose for his life. The Bible says:

> God has told us his secret reason for sending Christ, a plan he decided on in mercy long ago; and this was his purpose: that when the time is ripe he will gather us all together from wherever we are—in heaven or on earth—to be with him in Christ, forever. Moreover, because of what Christ has done we have become gifts to God that he delights in, for as part of God's sovereign plan we were chosen from the beginning to be his, and all things happen just as he decided long ago. God's purpose in this was that we should praise God and give glory to him for doing these mighty things for us, who were the first to trust in Christ (Ephesians 1:9–12, TLB).

Blaise Pascal, French physicist and philosopher, wrote in Penseé 425:

> The was once in man a true happiness of which there now remains only the mark and empty trace which he in vain tries to fill from all his surroundings... But these are all inadequate because the infinite abyss can only be filled... by God Himself.

Perhaps, in the quiet of your own heart, you are saying, "Yes, there is an emptiness; I am not satisfied with my life."

None of us can truly be fulfilled until we invite Christ to show us the purpose for which He created us. No one else who ever lived can do this for us—no religion, no philosophy, no man—but Jesus of Nazareth who is God in the flesh, perfect God and perfect man.

Jesus said:

> I am the way and the truth and the life. No one comes to the Father except through me (John 14:6).

As you come to know Him, He will show you that purpose for which He created you.

Jesus Alone Gives Peace

Jesus alone can *pardon* us from our sins. Jesus alone can give us *purpose* to life. And Jesus of Nazareth is the only one who can give us unshakable *peace* in a world of turmoil, for He is the Prince of Peace.

There will never be agreement at the peace tables of the world or rest in the individual heart until the Prince of Peace reigns supreme in the hearts of men.

What kind of peace does He give to those who trust Him? It is a sense of inner calm and security in the midst of trials, temptations, heartaches, and sorrows. It is a quiet confidence that, since our sovereign, loving, all-powerful God is in control, we have nothing to fear.

Everyone experiences difficulties. The Christian is not exempt. Receiving Jesus Christ as Savior does not mean that we will suddenly be ushered into a problem-free life. But, as followers of Jesus, you and I can rest in the promise He gave to all believers:

> I am leaving you with a gift—peace of mind and heart!
> And the peace I give isn't fragile like the peace the world
> gives. So don't be troubled or afraid (John 14:27, TLB).

Some years ago I was asked to speak at a meeting that was part of the famous Presidential Prayer Breakfast in Washington, D. C., sponsored by the International Christian Leadership Conference. In attendance was a young naval commander representing the Pentagon who happened to be an old fraternity brother and debate colleague of mine during our college days. When Frank saw my name on the program, he sought me out.

As we reminisced, he told me the story of the recent tragic loss of his child. As he shared his grief, he asked if I would accompany him to his home to talk with him and his dear wife. I immediately agreed.

As we shared together that evening, they both received Jesus Christ as their Savior and Lord. As they prayed, Jesus came into their lives, and they experienced a wonderful peace. Their lives were truly changed.

The following year I returned to Washington where I again participated in the Presidential Prayer Breakfast meetings. Frank was also present again, and he greeted me warmly.

With tears in his eyes, he told me that shortly after our previous visit, another of their children had become ill. She had cancer of the nervous system, which resulted in her death.

I shall never forget that day as Frank shared his heart with me. With a warm smile, he said, "As dearly as we loved our little angel and as much as we hated to see her go, during the time of her illness and after she was gone, the presence of the Lord Jesus Christ was so real! We do not understand it, but through it all we have continued to experience an incredible peace."

Many heartaches, sorrows, and problems will come into your life. But Christ, the Prince of Peace, wants to give you His pardon, His purpose, and His peace to help you live joyfully and abundantly.

Jesus also waits to fill you with another supernatural resource—His inexhaustible resurrection *power*—with which you can receive moment-by-moment strength and wisdom to live fruitfully and victoriously.

Jesus Alone Gives Power

Frequently, someone will say to me, "I'd like to become a Christian, but if I do, I'm sure I'll never be able to live the life. You don't know the mistakes I've made, the resentments I have, the tendencies to sin, the immorality, the heavy drinking, the cruel tongue, and many, many other problems. I don't believe I could live the Christian life."

But as these people have given their lives to Christ, they have discovered that the Christian life is a supernatural one.

As a young man in college and later in business I believed a person could do just about anything he wanted through his own self-effort if he was willing to pay the price of hard work and sacrifice. Then when I became a Christian, the Bible introduced me to a whole new philosophy of life—a life of trusting God, claiming His promises, and obeying His commands.

But I still did not understand that I lacked power to be what God wanted. Instead, I just changed the direction of my self-effort. I resorted to all kinds of self-imposed disciplines, including frequent fasting, much prayer, and good works. But the more I tried to live a victorious life, the more defeated and frustrated I became.

One day I read a passage in the book of Romans that says:

> The old sinful nature within us is against God. It never did obey God's laws and it never will (Romans 8:7, TLB).

In that same chapter I also read:

> The power of the life-giving Spirit—and this power is mine through Christ Jesus—has freed me from the vicious circle of sin and death (Romans 8:2, TLB).

What a relief to discover that I would never be able to live the Christian life through my own efforts, but that I could trust Christ to live His resurrection life in and through me by the power of His Holy Spirit! As I surrendered control of my life to the Lord Jesus, I felt liberated. Faith in God replaced my old attitude of self-sufficiency or faith in myself.

Through the years I have discovered just how weak I am in my own strength, and yet how strong I am in Christ. I began to understand what Jesus meant when he said:

> I am the vine; you are the branches. Whoever lives in
> me and I in him shall produce a large crop of fruit. For
> apart from me, you can't do a thing (John 15:5, TLB).

Indeed, Jesus of Nazareth is the only one who can give you and me power to live a new and more meaningful life. Because He literally comes to dwell within us through His Spirit, He will (as we invite Him) live the Christian life in and through us. Therefore, it is no longer what we do, but what He does. Because He provides the power, we are simply the instruments through which He re-

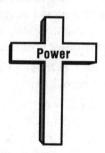

leases His strength. Paul describes this kind of relationship in Galatians 2:20:

> I have been crucified with Christ: and I myself no
> longer live, but Christ lives in me. And the real life I now
> have within this body is a result of my trusting in the Son
> of God, who loved me and gave himself for me (TLB).

I can identify with Paul who writes:

> Brothers, think of what you were when you were
> called. Not many of you were influential; not many were
> of noble birth. But God chose the foolish things of the
> world to shame the wise; God chose the weak things of
> the world to shame the strong. He chose the lowly things
> of this world and the despised things—and the things
> that are not—to nullify the things that are, so that no one
> may boast before him (1 Corinthians 1:26–29).

> Therefore I will boast all the more gladly about my
> weaknesses, so that Christ's power may rest on me (2
> Corinthians 12:9).

Making a Commitment

Experiencing God's pardon, purpose, peace, and power in our life requires total commitment to Jesus Christ.

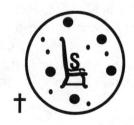

There is a throne in your life, and either Christ is on that throne or you are on it. If you say "I am the master of my life; I will do as I please," quite likely you are not a Christian. If Christ is on that throne, He has brought you back into relationship with Himself. In the Scriptures He says:

> Here I am! I stand at the door and knock [the door of your heart, your will, your intellect, your emotions]. If anyone hears my voice and opens the door, I will come in and eat with him, and he with me (Revelation 3:20).

> To all who receive him, to those who believed in his name, he gave the right to become children of God (John 1:12).

> If anyone is in Christ, he is a new creation; the old has gone, the new has come (2 Corinthians 5:17).

Commitment to Christ involves the surrender of the intellect, the emotions, and the will—the total person.

Let us say for the sake of illustration that you had heard many fine compliments about a certain person of the opposite sex. You could hardly wait to meet that person. The actual meeting was even more exciting. Intellectually you liked what you saw. You admired his looks and his personality; you liked everything about him. Was this enough to launch a marriage? No. There is more to marriage than mutual respect and admiration.

As you spent more and more time together, you became better acquainted. Then it happened. Cupid found his mark, and you were in love. Is this marriage? No. There is more to marriage than the intellect and the emotions. One day you become engaged and the wedding day arrives. How exciting!

Intellectually, you believe that he or she is the most wonderful person in all of the world. Emotionally, your heart beats twice as fast when you are together, but now something even more important is about to take place. As the two of you exchange vows before the minister, you commit your *wills*, one to the other. The marriage is not a true marriage if there is no mutual giving of one to the other. *There you have it. A marriage relationship involves the intellect, the emotions, and the will.*

So it is in becoming a Christian. One must give himself wholly to Christ: intellect, emotions, and will.

You may have heard someone say, "I believe that Jesus Christ is the Son of God. I believe that He died for my sins. Why, I have believed this all of my life. Am I not a Christian?" Not if that person has refused to yield his will to Him.

Another may say, "I remember when I heard a wonderful sermon at a youth retreat [or during a special series of meetings in our church]. My heart was stirred, and I had a great emotional experience. I even responded to the invitation to go forward for counsel. Am I not a Christian?" Not if that person has never relinquished the throne of his life—his will—to Christ.

Still another may say, "I go to church regularly; I read my Bible and pray daily. I try to live a good life. Am I not a Christian?" Not unless he has surrendered his will to Christ.

The surrender of the will is the key to becoming a Christian and the secret to living a victorious Christian life.

An outstanding young athlete and social leader wanted to become a Christian, but like so many, he was afraid to surrender his will to the will of God. He had worked out detailed plans for his life but was reluctant to become a Christian for fear God would change those plans.

As we talked together, I explained that God loved him dearly—so much that He sent His only begotten Son to die on the cross for his sins and that God had a wonderful plan for his life. I asked, "Don't you think you can trust someone who loves you this much and who is infinitely wiser than any of us?"

"I hadn't thought of it that way," he said. "I will trust Him."

As we prayed together, he invited Christ into his heart as Savior and Lord. Yes, his life was changed. And he is now devoting all of his time to challenging others to become Christians also. Since then, tens of thousands of young people and many of their parents have been influenced for Christ through his godly life and witness.

Your Invitation to Life

People in all walks and stages of life are discovering the pardon, purpose, peace, and power that only Christ can give. On thousands of occasions, with students, executives, leaders in government and the media, with rich and poor, old and young, I have had the privilege of introducing many to Christ. I have seen their joy and excitement.

Have you discovered the joy and peace of knowing Jesus Christ personally? Perhaps you have believed in the existence of God and His Son and have tried to live a good life. Maybe you have been baptized and are an active member of a church. But have you ever consciously invited Jesus Christ to take up residence within you, to forgive your sins and change your life? Have you surrendered your life to Him?

No matter who you are, at this very moment, you too can have the experience of a lifetime. Right now Jesus is knocking at the door of your heart. He offers you His wonderful love and plan for your life. He has already paid the penalty for your sins. He is asking you, in the quiet of your heart, to surrender your all to Him—your intellect, your emotions, and your will.

I urge you to invite Jesus Christ to come into your life to pardon your sins and live His life through you. Although He is "not willing that any should perish" (2 Peter 3:9, TLB), He will not force His way. He will enter your life only by your personal invitation.

God knows your heart and is not so concerned with your words as He is with your attitude.

If you want to receive Him as Savior and Lord, bow your head and pray this prayer or a similar one right now:

Lord Jesus, thank You for dying on the cross for my sins. I open the door of my life and receive You as my Savior and Lord. Thank You for forgiving my sins and giving me eternal life. Take control of the throne of my life. Make me the kind of person You want me to be. Amen.

If you prayed this prayer sincerely with your heart, Christ is now in your life. Your sins are forgiven. You are a child of God. You now have eternal life. Can you think of anything more wonderful? Take a moment right now to thank God in prayer for what He has done for you. By thanking Him, you demonstrate your faith.

If you have invited Jesus Christ into your life, you can have confidence that He is in your life and has given you eternal life as He promised. Jesus would not deceive you. You can be sure, if you asked Him into your life, that He now lives inside you and will give you the abundant life He promised.

As a new believer in Christ, you are ready to embark on the adventure of a lifetime to discover true purpose, peace, and power for living. In the process, you will find indescribable contentment through your relationship with Christ and enjoy the fulfilling, abundant, victorious, and fruitful life that He has promised every believer who trusts and obeys Him.

I encourage you to study the Word of God, the Bible, diligently and to become active in the vital Christian fellowship of a local church. The *Ten Basic Steps Toward Christian Maturity* have helped thousands of students and adults to a more vital and fruitful relationship with Christ. Daily study of this material will prove rewarding to you also. May God bless you and keep you in this great adventure with Christ our Savior.

Who Is Jesus Christ?

What if you could predict that a major world event would take place five minutes from now?

What if you could accurately describe what would happen?

Would knowing the future give you unusual power?

Would anyone believe you?

Possibly some would, but how many would not?

Many people do not believe the Bible, yet it miraculously foretells hundreds of events, sometimes in minute detail, and usually hundreds—sometimes thousands—of years ahead. Some prophecies concern cities and countries, such as Tyre, Jericho, Samaria, Jerusalem, Palestine, Moab, and Babylon. Others relate to specific individuals. Many have already been fulfilled, but some are still in the future.

Jesus Christ is the subject of more than 300 Old Testament prophecies. His birth nearly 2,000 years ago, and events of His life, had been foretold by many prophets during a period of 1,500 years. History confirms that even the smallest detail happened just as

Objective: To recognize Jesus Christ as the Son of God

Read: John 1:1–34

Memorize: John 14:6

predicted. It confirms beyond a doubt that Jesus is the true Messiah, the Son of God and Savior of the world.

The following chart lists some of the amazing predictions concerning Jesus Christ, together with the record of their fulfillment:

EVENT	OLD TESTAMENT PROPHECY	FULFILLMENT IN JESUS
His birth	Isaiah 7:14	Matthew 1:18,22,23
His birthplace	Micah 5:2	Luke 2:4,6,7
His childhood in Egypt	Hosea 11:1	Matthew 2:14,15
The purpose for His death	Isaiah 53:4–6	2 Corinthians 5:21 1 Peter 2:24
His betrayal	Zechariah 11:12,13; 13:6	Matthew 26:14–16; 27:3–10
His crucifixion	Psalm 22	Matthew 27
His resurrection	Psalm 16:9,10	Acts 2:31

Bible Study

Jesus' Claims Concerning Who He Is

1. In your own words, write the claims Christ made concerning Himself in the following verses:

    Mark 14:61,62

    John 6:38; 8:42

John 5:17,18

John 10:30

What did those who heard what Jesus said think He meant?

John 14:7

John 14:8,9

2. What did Jesus claim to do in the following verses?
John 5:22

Matthew 9:6

John 6:45–47

3. What did Jesus predict in the following verses?
Mark 9:31

Luke 18:31–33

John 14:1–3

4. What characteristics of Jesus are attributes of an
omnipotent God?
John 2:24

Matthew 8:26,27

John 11:43–45

According to the above passages, Jesus claimed to be God.
He made the kinds of claims that only a person who presumed
he was God would make. Both His friends and His enemies
called Him God, and He never attempted to deny it. He even
commended His followers for believing He was God.

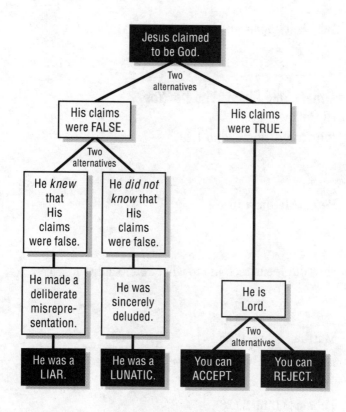

The Importance of the Truth About His Identity

1. Suppose Jesus Christ were not God. If He knew He was not God and that none of those claims were true, what could we conclude about Him?

2. Suppose Jesus were sincerely wrong. Suppose He sincerely believed all these fantastic claims, even though they were not true. What could we conclude about Him?

3. Why is it important to investigate His claims?

What Others Said About Who He Was

1. His followers:
   John the Baptist (John 1:29)

   Peter (Matthew 16:16)

   How did Jesus respond to what Peter said (verse 17)?

   Martha (John 11:27)

   Thomas (John 20:28)

   How does Christ's response to what Thomas said
   (verse 29) apply to you?

   Paul (2 Corinthians 5:21; Titus 2:13)

2. His enemies:
The Jews (John 10:33)

Judas (Matthew 27:3,4)

Pilate (Matthew 27:22,23)

The Roman soldier (Matthew 27:54)

3. Who do *you* believe Jesus is and on what do you base that belief? List the facts that particularly help you know that He is God.

LIFE APPLICATION

1 Why is it important that you personally recognize who Jesus Christ really is?

2 Have you invited Jesus Christ into your life? (See "Your Invitation to Life" on page 33.)

3 What changes do you expect to experience in your life as a result of receiving Christ as your Savior and Lord?

❖   ❖   ❖

The Earthly Life of Jesus Christ

Jesus Christ is the greatest person who ever lived. His moral character, His teachings, and His influence upon history demonstrate that He is indeed God. Through two thousand years of advancements in education, technology, philosophy, medicine, and science, mankind has never produced a person who is worthy to be compared with Jesus.

His divinity and humanity are without parallel. His life, death, and resurrection were mandatory for man's salvation. With His ascension into heaven, He completed His mission and made possible man's restoration to his original destiny.

Bible Study

Objective: To recognize that Christ's earthly life confirmed His deity

Read: John 17

Memorize: John 1:12

The Entrance of Jesus Christ Into the World

1. On the basis of His statement in John 17:5, where was Jesus Christ before He came into the world?

43

2. Read Matthew 1:18–23. In your own words, summarize the circumstances that surrounded Jesus' birth.

The New Testament passes over the next thirty years of Jesus' life almost in silence. Apparently the gospel writers were more anxious to portray the character and ministry of Jesus than to give us a chronological biography.

The Character of Jesus

1. From these verses, describe the character of Jesus:

Mark 1:40–42

Luke 23:33,34

John 2:13–17

John 13:1–17

Romans 5:8–10

2. How does Jesus' attitude contrast with the attitude of His contemporaries toward the following?
Adults (Matthew 14:15–21)

Children (Mark 10:13–16)

Those who offend (Luke 9:51–56)

3. Why did the following people love Christ?
The widow of Nain (Luke 7:11–15)

The sinful woman (Luke 7:36–50)

Mary and Martha (John 11:30–44)

4. From the beginning of His life, Jesus demonstrated unfailing grace, amazing wisdom, and astounding understanding and knowledge. He consistently pleased God.

The crowds found His compassion constant, and He was humble and meek before His enemies. He treated the poor with respect and the children with love and tenderness. His character was pure, selfless, and sinless.

Jesus also proved His divine character through His immeasurable love, an unconditional love unique in history. He willingly offered Himself as a sacrifice for all sin and evil, and He gave the free gift of everlasting life to every person who would accept it. Only God in the flesh could have embodied all these characteristics.

Read Hebrews 4:15. How can Jesus understand our feelings so completely?

According to Luke 2:42–47, when did Jesus first demonstrate His depth of knowledge and commitment?

What was the general reaction to Jesus' remarks?

5. Read Matthew 7:28,29. What other reactions do you think the people had to His teachings besides amazement?

Imagine yourself in Jesus' day, listening to Him teach and observing His behavior. What would your reaction be?

6. How do you feel about Jesus?

Why?

Jesus Christ as a Teacher

1. What did Christ teach about the new birth (John 3:1–8)?

Why did He describe salvation in this way?

2. What did Christ teach regarding His claims about Himself?
John 10:11

John 13:13,14

John 15:1,5

Matthew 5:17

John 11:25,26

Which of these claims do you think is most important?

Why?

Which has meant the most to you personally?

Why?

3. What did Christ teach about His demands of His followers?
Mark 8:38

Mark 10:29,30

Matthew 9:9

Matthew 11:29

Luke 9:23

John 13:34,35

Which of these demands do you find easiest to follow?

How do you think Jesus wants you to deal with the difficult ones?

4. Many view Jesus as the greatest teacher in history. No other man has been quoted as often or has inspired as many books and articles. His teachings have given us clear, profound insights into the deepest questions of life. People flocked to hear Him speak. The disciples left everything to follow Him. What kind of teacher could inspire such loyalty? (See John 6:66–69 for help in formulating your answer.)

From the following verses, list characteristics of Jesus that made Him such an excellent teacher:

Mark 6:34

Luke 21:29–38

Luke 4:14–30

John 3:1–8; 7:50,51; 19:38–42

5. Carefully read Matthew 7:7–12 from the Sermon on the Mount. How did Jesus use the following teaching methods to emphasize His lessons?

Repetition of ideas

Practical application

Clear summarization

6. What was even more important than Christ's effective teaching methods (Matthew 7:29)?

Where did He get this authority (John 12:49,50)?

Summarize how Jesus' earthly life confirmed His deity.

LIFE APPLICATION

1 Give at least three reasons you can trust Jesus'
teachings:

1)

2)

3)

2 List three ways these teachings can change your life:

1)

2)

3)

3 Plan how you will implement these changes.

LESSON 3

The Death of Jesus Christ

When did you last talk about death? Did you enjoy your conversation?

People don't usually like to talk about death, do they? But the Bible has some very important things to say about it.

According to God's Word, death means "separation," not "cessation of existence." Physical death is the separation of the spirit (the immaterial part of us) from the body. As a result, the body decomposes. Spiritual death is the separation of man from God. Both physical and spiritual death are the results of sin.

The results of this separation are not only sins like murder, immorality, and stealing, but also worry, irritability, lack of purpose in life, frustration, the desire to escape reality, and fear of death. These and many other conditions are evidence that we are cut off from God, the only One who can give us the power to live an abundant life.

The most important question in life becomes, "How can I be reconciled to God?" In our own power, we can never bridge the gulf between us and God. But God has provided a way to bring us to Him.

Objective: To understand the meaning of Christ's death on the cross and the importance of receiving Him as Savior and Lord

Read: Romans 3:10–28; 5:1–21

Memorize: Romans 5:8

Bible Study

The Need for the Death of Jesus Christ

1. Carefully read Romans 3:10–12 and 3:23.

How many times does the writer, Paul, use terms like *all, none,* or their equivalents?

Why do you think he repeats these terms?

What does this tell you about moral, respectable people?

2. What is the result of sin (Romans 6:23)?

The Result of the Death of Christ

1. Read 2 Corinthians 5:21 carefully.
How good does it say Christ was?

But what happened to Him when He died on the cross to pay the penalty of our sins?

What was the result for you?

2. What did Christ teach concerning His death
(Mark 8:31,32)?

3. How did Christ feel about such a death (Hebrews 12:2)?

4. Describe the effect of Christ's death with respect to
God's holiness (Romans 3:25; John 4:10).

5. Why did He die for us (1 Peter 3:18)?

6. How did Christ's death affect your relationship with God
(Colossians 1:21,22; Romans 5:10,11)?

Significance of the Death of Christ

1. What is the only thing we can do to make sure that
the death of Christ applies to us so we can be saved
(Acts 16:31)?

2. Can we work for salvation (Ephesians 2:8,9)?

Why not?

LIFE APPLICATION

1 Read John 3:18 carefully. What two kinds of people are described here?

2 What is the only reason any person will be condemned?

3 According to what the Bible says here, are you condemned?

4 According to 1 John 5:11,12, do you have eternal life? (Do not confuse 1 John, the Epistle, near the end of the New Testament, with the Gospel of John.)

5 According to that same passage, how can you know?

6 Have you made the decision to accept Christ's death on the cross for you, and have you received Him into your life as Savior and Lord? If you would like to receive Him as your Savior right now, pray a prayer like this one from your heart:

> *Lord Jesus, I want to know you personally. Thank You for dying on the cross for my sins. I open the door of my life and receive You as my Savior and Lord. Thank You for forgiving my sins and giving me eternal life. Make me the kind of person You want me to be. Amen.*

The Resurrection of Jesus Christ

Jesus' crucifixion demoralized His followers. The terror-stricken little band scattered; Jesus' enemies were celebrating their victory. But three days after the crucifixion a miracle occurred: Jesus rose from the dead.

Within a few weeks His once cowardly followers were fearlessly proclaiming His resurrection, a fact that changed the course of history. Followers of Jesus Christ were not people who promoted an ethical code of a dead founder, but rather those who had had vital contact with a living Lord. Jesus Christ still lives today, and He is anxiously waiting to work in the lives of those who will trust Him.

The new life and fresh courage demonstrated by the early Christians is vividly described by J. B. Phillips in the Preface to his *Letters to Young Churches:*

> The great difference between present-day Christianity and that of which we read in these letters is that to us it is primarily a performance; to them it was a real experience. We are apt to reduce the Christian religion to a code, or at best a rule of heart and life. To these men it is quite plainly the invasion of their lives by a new quality of life al-

Objective: To recognize the importance of Christ's resurrection, and how it relates to us personally

Read: John 20

Memorize: 1 Corinthians 15:3,4

together. They do not hesitate to describe this as Christ "living in" them.

Mere moral reformation will hardly explain the transformation and the exuberant vitality of these men's lives—even if we could prove a motive for such reformation, and certainly the world around offered little encouragement to the early Christian! We are practically driven to accept their own explanation, which is that their little human lives had, through Christ, been linked up with the very life of God.

Many Christians today talk about the "difficulties of our times" as though we should have to wait for better ones before the Christian religion can take root. It is heartening to remember that this faith took root and flourished amazingly in conditions that would have killed anything less vital in a matter of weeks.

These early Christians were on fire with the conviction that they had become, through Christ, literal sons of God; they were pioneers of a new humanity, founders of a new kingdom.

They still speak to us across the centuries. Perhaps if we believed what they believed, we might achieve what they achieved.

Bible Study

Five Proofs That Jesus Actually Rose From the Dead

1. *The resurrection was foretold by Jesus Christ, the Son of God.*
What did Jesus tell His disciples in Luke 18:31–33?

If Jesus had clearly predicted that He would rise from the dead, then failed to do so, what would this say about Him?

2. *The resurrection of Christ is the only reasonable explanation for the empty tomb.*

What did Jesus' friends do to make certain His body would not be taken (Mark 15:46)?

What did Jesus' enemies do to make sure His body would not be taken (Matthew 27:62–66)?

But on Sunday morning the tomb was *empty!*

   Note: If Jesus had not been killed, but only weakened and wounded by crucifixion, the stone and the soldiers would have prevented His escape from the tomb. If Jesus' friends had tried to steal His body, the stone and the soldiers would likewise have prevented them. Jesus' enemies would never have taken the body since its absence from the tomb would only serve to encourage belief in His resurrection. *Only His resurrection can account for the empty tomb!*

3. *The resurrection is the only reasonable explanation for the appearance of Jesus Christ to His disciples.*

List all the individuals or groups who actually saw the risen Christ, according to 1 Corinthians 15:4–8:

If Christ had not risen from the dead, what could we then conclude about all these witnesses (1 Corinthians 15:15)?

What else would be true if Christ had not risen from the dead (1 Corinthians 15:17)?

When Christ appeared to His followers, what things did He do to prove He was not a hallucination (Luke 24:36-43)?

4. *The dramatic change in the lives of His followers.*
Look up these verses and describe the differences in these people:
Peter (Luke 22:54–62; Acts 4:1–22)

Thomas (John 20:24–28; Acts 1:12–14)

Paul (Acts 7:54–8:3; Acts 16:16–40)

5. *The resurrection is the only reasonable explanation for the beginning of the Christian church.*
Within a few weeks after Jesus' resurrection, Peter preached at Pentecost, and the Christian church began. What was the subject of his sermon (Acts 2:14–36)?

If Jesus' body were still in the tomb, how do you think Peter's audience would have responded to this sermon?

But how did they respond (Acts 2:37,38,41,42)?

The Results of the Resurrection

1. What does the resurrection tell us about the following: Jesus Christ (Romans 1:4)

The power God can now exercise in our lives (Ephesians 1:19,20)

What will eventually happen to our bodies (Philippians 3:21)

2. How would your life be affected if Christ had not risen from the dead (1 Corinthians 15:12–26)?

3. If we can believe the resurrection, why is it then logical to believe all the miracles Jesus performed?

The Visible Return of Christ

1. Describe the way in which Christ will return to earth
   (Matthew 24:30; Acts 1:11).

2. How does this compare to the first time Christ came
   to earth?

3. What will happen to the Christian when Christ comes for
   him (1 Corinthians 15:51,52; Philippians 3:20,21)?

4. What will be the condition of the earth when Christ returns
   (Matthew 24:6–8)?

5. What will happen to those who are not Christians when
   He returns (2 Thessalonians 1:7–9)?

6. What is our present hope (1 John 2:2,3)?

LIFE APPLICATION

Hebrews 13:8 says Jesus is the same today, and He can transform your life.

1 How would your life be different from what it is if Jesus had not risen from the dead?

2 How do you think His "resurrection life" can be seen in you on a daily basis?

3 How can your life be different if you allow Jesus to transform it?

❖   ❖   ❖

Jesus Christ Living in the Christian

Objective: To realize the importance of total surrender to Christ

Read: Revelation 2 and 3

Memorize: Revelation 3:20

Are you a member of a church? Are you committed and active in your church? And do you have a close relationship with Jesus Christ?

Chapters 2 and 3 of Revelation emphasize the fact that merely to be a church member offers no guarantee of a right relationship with Jesus Christ. Notice in Revelation 3:20 that the reference is to individuals, not to a group as a whole: "If anyone hears my voice and opens the door, I will go in and eat with him, and he with me."

When you invite Jesus Christ to come into your heart and life to be your Savior and Lord, confessing your sin and need of forgiveness, He answers your prayer. He enters your heart and life. Why?

One reason is so He can empower you. The Christian life is more than difficult; it is humanly impossible to live. Only Jesus Christ can live it through you as He dwells within you. He wants to think with your mind, express Himself through your emotions, and speak through your voice, though you may be unconscious of it.

But as worldly Christians examine their lives, they often find themselves filled with many areas of activity—studies, finances, social life, home life, business, travel—but with no real purpose or meaning. The reason for this is that they are controlling these areas themselves instead of allowing Jesus Christ to control them.

There is a throne in each of our lives (see diagram below). Until Jesus Christ comes into our lives, our self, or ego, is on the throne. But when Jesus comes in, He wants to assume His place of authority on this throne. We must step down and relinquish the authority of our lives to Him. As you can see from the diagram, when Christ becomes the controller of our lives, He becomes Lord of every activity, and that results in purpose and harmony.

Thus the Christian life is not a person trying to imitate Christ; rather, it is Christ imparting His life to and living His life through the person. The Christian life is not what you do for Him; it is what He does for and through you. The Christ-controlled life always produces the fruit of the Spirit as listed in Galatians 5:22,23.

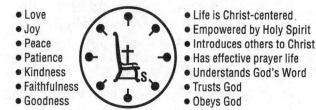

• Love		• Life is Christ-centered
• Joy		• Empowered by Holy Spirit
• Peace		• Introduces others to Christ
• Patience		• Has effective prayer life
• Kindness		• Understands God's Word
• Faithfulness		• Trusts God
• Goodness		• Obeys God

❖

Bible Study

The Need for Jesus Christ to Live in the Christian

1. What was Jesus unwilling to entrust to men (John 2:24,25)?

Why?

2. What kinds of things are in our hearts (Mark 7:21–23)?

3. How did the apostle Paul, one of the world's greatest Christians, evaluate his human nature (Romans 7:18)?

4. What is our condition apart from Jesus Christ (John 15:4,5)?

The Fact that Jesus Christ Lives in the Christian

1. Restate Revelation 3:20 in your own words:

Note: The word *sup* that appears in some translations is Old English for "eat" or "dine," and it describes the idea of fellowship in its original meaning.

2. What guarantee does Jesus Christ give in this verse, and how can we believe Him?

3. How do you know that Jesus Christ has entered your life?

4. How do you know that Jesus will never leave you even when you sin (Hebrews 13:5)?

5. If you do sin, how can you renew your fellowship with Him (1 John 1:9)?

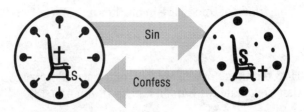

Note: *Salvation* differs from *fellowship*. Salvation is having our sins forgiven and receiving eternal life. Fellowship is our daily relationship, or communion, with Christ. Through sin we may often lose our fellowship in the same way a child loses fellowship with his father through disobedience. However, the child does not lose his relationship as a son, nor do we lose our relationship with God. He is still our heavenly Father. (See John 10:27-29.)

Jesus Christ at Home Within the Christian

When Jesus Christ lives within us, what can He do for us as we face the following problems?

 1. Emptiness (John 6:35)

 2. Anxiety (John 14:27)

 3. Unhappiness (John 15:11)

 4. Lack of power (Philippians 4:13)

LIFE APPLICATION

1 What must we do so that Jesus Christ can live His victorious life through us (Romans 6:13; 12:1,2)?

2 Read and meditate on John 3:16. On the basis of this verse, why do you think we should give control of our lives to God?

3 Right now, surrender control of your life to God. Be willing to give Him every area—your family, job, finances, even your health. Pray this simple prayer:

Dear Father, I need You. I acknowledge that I have been directing my own life and that, as a result, I have sinned against You. I thank You for forgiving my sins through Christ's death on the cross for me. I now invite Christ to again take His place on the throne of my life. Fill me with the Holy Spirit as You commanded me to be filled in Ephesians 5:18, and as You promised in Your Word that You would do if I ask in faith. I now thank You for directing my life and for filling me with the Holy Spirit. Amen.

❖ ❖ ❖

The Church of Jesus Christ

What is the strongest organization on earth? It is the church. Composed of every person who has received Jesus Christ into his or her life, the church is also called the Body of Christ or the Bride of Christ. It is the one organization for which He gave His life (Ephesians 5:25).

The Bible describes the church in two senses:

1) The universal church, which refers to all true Christians

2) The local church, which is an individual group of Christians who gather for worship, instruction, and mutual encouragement

Objective: To recognize the importance of the church in the Christian's life

Read: Hebrews 10:19–25; 1 Corinthians 12:12–31

Memorize: Hebrews 10:25

Bible Study

The Universal Church

1. Paul frequently compares the church to a body. Who is the only head (Ephesians 5:23)?

Who are the members (1 Corinthians 12:27)?

2. How does Christ see the church (1 Corinthians 12:12,13)?

3. As members of His body, how should we feel toward each other (1 Corinthians 12:25,26)?

Name some specific ways we can express these feelings.

4. Read Acts 1:6–11 carefully.
According to verse 8, what is to be the church's great concern?

Where does the Bible say Jesus went physically (verse 9)?

Describe in your own words how Jesus will come again for His church (verse 11).

Who knows when that will be (verse 7)? (See also
Mark 13:32,33.)

Although Jesus is spiritually present in our hearts, He is also
with God the Father in heaven. In the future, He will return
to judge the world and rule the nations (Matthew 25:31,32).
In the meantime, the church is to be His witness on earth and
bring as many people as possible into a personal relationship
with Him.

5. In light of this, what should be one of your main purposes
while here on earth?

The Local Church

1. What are Christians *not* to do (Hebrews 10:25)?

Note: The "meeting together" refers to the regular assembling
of the local church.

2. We are saved by faith. But the church has two simple, yet
meaningful, ordinances that we are to observe: baptism and
communion.

According to Matthew 28:18,19, why should we be baptized?

What is the purpose of the communion service (1 Corinthians 11:23–26)?

3. Write your own one-sentence description of each of the following local churches:

The church in Jerusalem (Acts 4:32,33)

The church in Thessalonica (1 Thessalonians 1:6–10)

The church in Laodicea (Revelation 3:14–17)

Just as some New Testament churches are dynamic and others powerless, so it is today. Not all churches are vital, and great variety exists even within a single denomination. To stimulate your Christian growth, you should attend a church that exalts Christ, teaches the Bible, explains clearly what a Christian is and how to become one, and provides loving fellowship.

4. What could happen to your spiritual growth if you:

Do not attend church regularly?

Attend a church that is powerless?

LIFE APPLICATION

❶ Give at least two reasons it is important for us to be a part of a local church.

1)

2)

❷ If you are not active in a local church, plan right now to get involved.

◆ Ask your Christian friends to recommend dynamic churches. Write the church names here:

◆ Pray over the list.
◆ Ask God to help you select the best one for you.
◆ Visit each until you prayerfully decide on one.
◆ Then look for ways to serve the Lord in your church.

❖ ❖ ❖

Recap

The following questions will help you review this Step. If necessary, reread the appropriate lesson(s).

1. List ways the memory verses have helped you in your daily life during the weeks of this study.

2. What do you think is the most important way in which Jesus Christ is different from other people?

Reread: John 1:1–34;
Romans 3:10–28;
Romans 5:1–21; John 20

Review: Verses
memorized

What does that mean to you?

75

How does it affect your life?

3. Who is Jesus Christ to you?

What has He given you?

4. Why do you suppose Jesus' enemies did not want to believe
His claims about who He was?

5. Why did Jesus' friends, who had watched Him die, believe
in the resurrection?

LIFE APPLICATION

1 What does it mean to you now to have Jesus living within you?

2 How does your present relationship with Christ help you develop a rich fellowship with your local church?

3 How can you improve your relationship with other Christians?

4 How does your fellowship in your church help your relationship with God?

5 Write down ways you could make the relationship more vital.

❖   ❖   ❖

Resources for a Deeper Study of Jesus Christ

Ten Basic Steps. A comprehensive curriculum for the Christian who wants to master the basics of Christian growth. Used by hundreds of thousands worldwide. (See page 79 for details.)

The Ten Basic Steps Leader's Guide. Contains Bible study outlines for teaching the complete series.

The Handbook for Christian Maturity. Combines the entire series of the *Ten Basic Steps* in one volume. A handy resource for private Bible study; an excellent book to help nurture spiritual growth and maturity.

A Man Without Equal. A fresh look at the unique birth, teachings, death, and resurrection of Jesus and how He continues to change the way we live and think. Good as an evangelistic tool.

Life Without Equal. A presentation of the length and breadth of the Christian's freedom in Jesus Christ and how believers can release Christ's resurrection power for life and ministry. Good for unbelievers or Christians who want to grow in their Christian life.

Five Steps of Christian Growth. Teaches new believers the five cornerstones of faith: assurance of salvation, understanding God's love, experiencing God's forgiveness, being filled with the Holy Spirit, and steps to growing in Christ.

Available through your local Christian bookstore, mail-order catalog distributor, or NewLife Publications.

Ten Basic Steps Toward Christian Maturity

Eleven easy-to-use individual guides to help you understand the basics of the Christian faith

INTRODUCTION:
The Uniqueness of Jesus

Explains who Jesus Christ is. Reveals the secret of His power to turn you into a victorious, fruitful Christian.

STEP 1: The Christian Adventure

Shows you how to enjoy a full, abundant, purposeful, and fruitful life in Christ.

STEP 2: The Christian and the Abundant Life

Explores the Christian way of life—what it is and how it works practically.

STEP 3: The Christian and the Holy Spirit

Teaches who the Holy Spirit is, how to be filled with the Spirit, and how to make the Spirit-filled life a moment-by-moment reality in your life.

STEP 4: The Christian and Prayer

Reveals the true purpose of prayer and shows how the Father, Son, and Holy Spirit work together to answer your prayers.

STEP 5: The Christian and the Bible

Talks about the Bible—how we got it, its authority, and its power to help the believer. Offers methods for studying the Bible more effectively.

STEP 6: The Christian and Obedience

Learn why it is so important to obey God and how to live daily in His grace. Discover the secret to personal purity and power as a Chris-

tian and why you need not fear what others think of you.

STEP 7: The Christian and Witnessing

Shows you how to witness effectively. Includes a reproduction of the *Four Spiritual Laws* and explains how to share them.

STEP 8: The Christian and Giving

Discover God's plan for your financial life, how to stop worrying about money, and how to trust God for your finances.

STEP 9: Exploring the Old Testament

Features a brief survey of the Old Testament. Shows what God did to prepare the way for Jesus Christ and the redemption of all who receive Him as Savior and Lord.

STEP 10: Exploring the New Testament

Surveys each of the New Testament books. Shows the essence of the gospel and highlights the exciting beginning of the Christian church.

Leader's Guide

The ultimate resource for even the most inexperienced, timid, and fearful person asked to lead a group study in the basics of the Christian life. Contains questions and answers from the *Ten Basic Steps* Study Guides.

A Handbook for Christian Maturity

Combines the eleven-booklet series into one practical, easy-to-follow volume. Excellent for personal or group study.

Available through your local Christian bookstore, mail-order catalog distributor, or NewLife Publications.

About the Author

BILL BRIGHT is founder and president of Campus Crusade for Christ International. Serving in 155 major countries representing 98 percent of the world's population, he and his dedicated associates of more than 113,000 full-time staff, associate staff, and trained volunteers have introduced tens of millions of people to Jesus Christ, discipling millions to live Spirit-filled, fruitful lives of purpose and power for the glory of God.

Dr. Bright did graduate study at Princeton and Fuller Theological seminaries from 1946 to 1951. The recipient of many national and international awards, including five honorary doctorates, he is the author of numerous books and publications committed to helping fulfill the Great Commission. His special focus is *NewLife2000*, an international effort to help reach more than six billion people with the gospel of our Lord Jesus Christ and help fulfill the Great Commission by the year 2000.